A Quilting Life
Planner and Workbook

YOUR HOW-TO GUIDE TO
GETTING (AND STAYING) ORGANIZED

SHERRI L. McCONNELL

Martingale
Create with Confidence

A Quilting Life Planner and Workbook:
Your How-to Guide to Getting (and Staying) Organized
© 2021 by Sherri L. McConnell

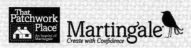

Martingale®
18939 120th Ave. NE, Ste. 101
Bothell, WA 98011-9511 USA
ShopMartingale.com

Printed in Hong Kong
26 25 24 23 22 21   8 7 6 5 4 3 2 1

**Library of Congress Cataloging-in-Publication Data
is available upon request.**

ISBN: 978-1-68356-158-3

MISSION STATEMENT

We empower makers who use fabric and yarn
to make life more enjoyable.

CREDITS

PUBLISHER AND CHIEF VISIONARY OFFICER
Jennifer Erbe Keltner

CONTENT DIRECTOR
Karen Costello Soltys

COPY EDITOR
Durby Peterson

DESIGN MANAGER
Adrienne Smitke

PRODUCTION MANAGER
Regina Girard

COVER AND BOOK DESIGNER
Angie Haupert Hoogensen

PHOTOGRAPHERS
Brent Kane
Adam Albright

Introduction

MY PASSIONS FOR SEWING, QUILTING, AND ORGANIZING GO HAND IN HAND. I've been fascinated by productivity, list-making, and organizational systems for keeping up with everything since I was young. As a quilter, I've enjoyed how this fascination has helped me get more done in my sewing and quilting life.

The framework for this planner and workbook came through years of my own experience, as well as from feedback from users of my previous planners and tools that I share on my website at AQuiltingLife.com. My hope is that you'll use this workbook and planner to take a more thorough look at your quilting life and organizing systems. For some of you, it will be another small step in your organizing journey. And for others, it might be a leap into the unknown— perhaps the first time you've tried to undertake an orderly approach to any area of your life that may seem somewhat overwhelming or out of control.

Either way, I know from experience that quilters who have a place to record their tools, notions patterns, and projects are more satisfied with how they manage their time and their progress. I've included lots of prompts throughout this workbook so you'll be able to customize these organizing principles to work with your life. I encourage you to start at the beginning and build your skills as you work through the planner month by month. Read ahead as you're inspired to do so, but don't skip over entire sections or you'll miss some of the progression. Best of all, you can start at any time, adding the month and dates for whichever time of year you're beginning.

This workbook is meant to help you gain a complete perspective of the systems and ideas that I've found most helpful. They're the ones I use myself. Even though organization isn't a "one size fits all" system, the basic principles included here will help you develop the ideal program for you. Happy organizing, planning, and sewing and quilting!

Sherri

⚙ LOOKING FOR MORE?
Visit my website at AQuiltingLife.com
for additional ideas and inspiration.

Contents

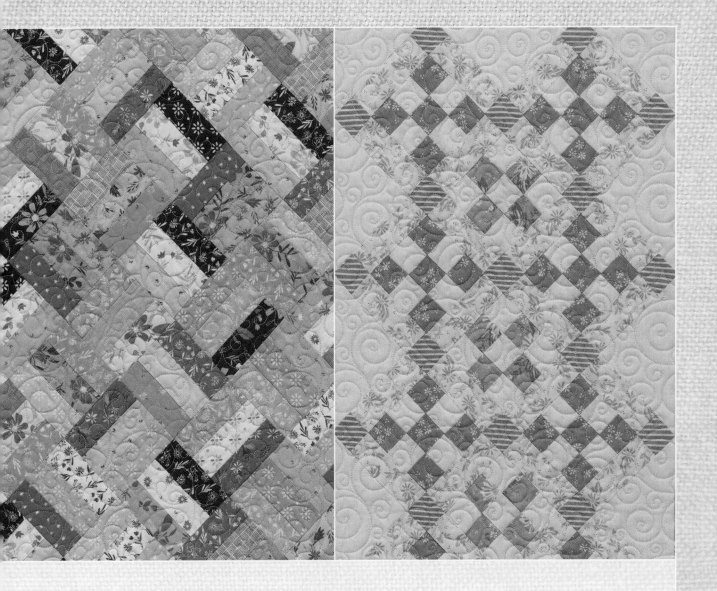

THE WAY TO GET STARTED IS TO QUIT TALKING AND BEGIN DOING. —WALT DISNEY

YOU'RE OFF TO GREAT PLACES!
TODAY IS YOUR DAY!
YOUR MOUNTAIN IS WAITING
SO . . . GET ON YOUR WAY!
—DR. SEUSS

REVIEW YOUR GOALS AND SCHEDULE TIME FOR:
- [ ] Works-in-Progress [ ] Long-Term Projects
- [ ] Organization [ ] [ ]

month

month

REFLECTION

Have you been a journal keeper off and on? Or committed to writing on a daily or weekly basis, then fallen out of the habit all too quickly? Maybe you've never thought about how important the process of reflecting can be as you make plans for the future. Well, change is ahead!

As a reader, have you enjoyed start-of-a-new-month blogs or end-of-the-year posts where writers share their progress and projects from the preceding month(s)? I always have. Putting that into quilting terms, I find that recapping the finishes and progress I make has become one of my traditions as well. If you've found yourself marveling at what others accomplish in a month or season, then consider reflecting on your accomplishments one of YOUR traditions too. You'll quickly notice just how good it feels to revel in what you've accomplished!

Reflection Exercises

Realizing the importance of reflection, the more you engage in it, you might decide to do some kind of reflection exercise on a weekly or biweekly basis. Personally, I take a bit more time for monthly, quarterly, and yearly reflections, but I do appreciate the boost to my self-confidence that comes from doing weekly reviews. Are you a list maker that loves to check a box or cross off a line on your to-do list? If you said *yes*, I can already feel the enthusiasm building for a few reflection exercises!

Let's begin with a review of your finishes and successes. Following that, answer the questions to focus on the things you aren't as happy with, and plan to turn them into wins in the future. Be sure to record your dreams and goals too.

WHAT WERE YOUR FAVORITE FINISHES OVER THE PAST WEEK? MONTH? QUARTER? YEAR?

WHY DO YOU LOVE THE FINISH(ES) THAT YOU LISTED AS FAVORITES? WAS IT THE PROCESS OR THE FINISHED PRODUCT THAT CAUSED YOU TO ADD THE ITEM(S) TO YOUR LIST? *Really ponder over this question and make notes as needed.*

TO BE YOURSELF IN A WORLD THAT IS CONSTANTLY TRYING TO MAKE YOU SOMETHING ELSE
IS THE GREATEST ACCOMPLISHMENT. —RALPH WALDO EMERSON

WHAT TYPES OF PROJECTS DO YOU WANT TO DO MORE OF IN THE COMING WEEKS, MONTHS, AND YEAR?

NOW SPEND SOME TIME THINKING ABOUT THE PROJECTS YOU *DIDN'T* LOVE AS MUCH AS THE ONES YOU'VE ALREADY COUNTED AS FAVORITES. WHAT TYPES OF PROJECTS DO YOU WANT TO DO LESS OF IN THE FUTURE? WHY?

IS THERE A PROJECT YOU MIGHT WANT TO DO THAT IS JUST A LITTLE MORE CHALLENGING? *(This might be a project to work on over a longer period of time. For this type of project, it's a good idea to have a few different ideas in mind. Think about trying one block or a simplified version first before embarking on a long-term challenge. Make notes here as you work through your ideas and come up with a list that excites you and maybe pushes you a wee bit outside of your comfort zone.)*

Reflecting on Current Organizational Systems

Later in this planner you'll find an entire section (page 77) that focuses on developing systems in your sewing and personal life that can improve your efficiency and time management. The next few questions present some prompts and ideas to reflect on so that you're ready to begin designing your own systems. Remember, there are no right or wrong answers here. Use these prompts to focus on areas that you currently have under control, as well as those areas you want to improve.

WRITE DOWN WHAT SYSTEMS, IF ANY, YOU HAVE IN PLACE WITH REGARDS TO QUILTING AND SEWING. INCLUDE WHAT WORKS WELL AND WHAT DOESN'T SEEM TO BE WORKING AS WELL.

TO ACCOMPLISH
GREAT THINGS,
WE MUST NOT ONLY ACT,
BUT ALSO DREAM;
NOT ONLY PLAN, BUT
ALSO BELIEVE.
—ANATOLE FRANCE

WRITE DOWN WHAT HOME-BASED SYSTEMS, IF ANY, YOU HAVE IN PLACE (MENU PLANNING, CLEANING, MAIL, PAPER TRACKING, CALENDARING, AND/OR TIME MANAGEMENT). INCLUDE YOUR THOUGHTS HERE ABOUT WHAT WORKS AND WHAT DOESN'T. ALSO CONSIDER HOW IMPORTANT IT IS FOR YOU TO WORK ON THESE SYSTEMS.

REVIEW YOUR GOALS AND SCHEDULE TIME FOR:

☐ Works-in-Progress ☐ Long-Term Projects
☐ Organization ☐ ☐

month

LOVE IT? LIST IT!

Makers are gonna make! And as makers, quilters often start more projects than they finish. To make sure projects aren't dropping off your radar, it's important to understand the different types of projects you have underway.

Projects you intend to finish in the short term might be current works-in-progress (WIPs) or unfinished objects (UFOs). Long-term projects are ones that might span the course of a year or more. And "Bucket List" projects are the ones you've been dreaming about making someday.

Making Lists

Separating different types of projects when listing or tracking them is an essential way to keep them from being forgotten or ignored. For that reason, you'll find separate spaces in this planner to record your notes about each of these types of projects. Listing the status of projects currently underway is a great first step toward developing systems (more on that later) to help you keep up with your varied projects over time.

Current Works-in-Progress

Gifts for the current year, block-of-the-month quilts, seasonal projects, and other short-term projects should all make their way onto your "Current Works-in-Progress" list. Consider the following as you work on your list of WIPs:

» Before adding a project to your current WIP list, consider whether it is indeed something you intend to finish in a year or less.

» It's much easier to work on a current project periodically if you store all of the needed items in a single bin or drawer so that everything is together when you're ready to work on it.

» If you get behind on a project with a scheduled timetable (block-of-the-month) or deadline (seasonal sew-along), jump back in at the pace of the larger group. For example, if you made block one but the group is beginning on block four this month, start with block four. You can finish blocks two and three later and enjoy the camaraderie of the group sew-along sharing your progress.

» If your pattern allows for it, sew blocks together into rows as you complete them. Doing so might make completing the project quicker and easier, or less daunting, at the end.

1. _____

FINISHED ☐

2. _____

FINISHED ☐

3. _____

FINISHED ☐

4. _____

FINISHED ☐

5. _____

FINISHED ☐

6. _____

FINISHED ☐

7.

FINISHED ☐

8.

FINISHED ☐

9.

FINISHED ☐

10.

FINISHED ☐

11.

FINISHED ☐

12.

FINISHED ☐

13.

FINISHED ☐

14.

FINISHED ☐

15.

FINISHED ☐

16.

FINISHED ☐

17.

FINISHED ☐

18.

FINISHED ☐

Long-Term Works-in-Progress

Not all projects were meant to be started and finished in short order. Consider long-term projects those that might take a year or more to complete. Perhaps you're making a scrap quilt that uses blocks from each project you made in a year. Or you might have a handwork or other more time-consuming project you're not in a rush to complete. Either way, this list is for those projects you want to linger over, enjoying the journey. Even so, it's a good idea to record these projects so they don't fall off your radar and out of mind in the rush of everyday living. Additionally, review the list regularly (try monthly or quarterly at a minimum) to ensure you make progress on these projects from time to time.

1. _____

   _____

   _____ FINISHED ☐

2. _____

   _____

   _____ FINISHED ☐

3. _____

   _____

   _____ FINISHED ☐

4. _____

   _____

   _____ FINISHED ☐

5. _____

   _____

   _____ FINISHED ☐

6. _____

   _____

   _____ FINISHED ☐

7. _____

   _____

   _____ FINISHED ☐

8. _____

   _____

   _____ FINISHED ☐

9. _____

   _____

   _____ FINISHED ☐

Bucket List Projects

We all have them—quilts we dream about making but haven't yet begun. They're the "someday" quilts you've thought about. When the time is right, they'll make it to your current WIPs or long-term WIPS lists, but until then it's fun to dream about what the future could hold. Make sure you capture your dreams on your "Bucket List" so you're ready when "someday" comes around.
Use this list as a handy reference for what you hope to make. List not only the project or pattern you're thinking of making but also color palette ideas and specialty tool location if you've already purchased those.

1.

2.

3.

4.

5.

6.

7.

8.

9.

REVIEW YOUR GOALS AND SCHEDULE TIME FOR:

☐ Works-in-Progress ☐ Long-Term Projects

☐ Organization ☐ _____ ☐ _____

month

QUILTING & SEWING SYSTEMS

In nearly every aspect of life, things run more smoothly when you have some kind of system in place to keep yourself on track. Learn more about the overall home organizing systems that I've found most effective later in this planner (page 77). But for this month, let's focus on quilting and sewing systems. Reflect on the questions that follow to help you get started. You'll also find some resources for putting your new systems into place. Note that some of the systems discussed this month will also have further content elsewhere in the planner as noted.

Systems for Current Works-in-Progress

FIRST, make a list of all of the current projects you're working on. You can record these projects starting on page 23.

NEXT, decide the time you have available to work on current projects. Perhaps you sew every evening for a couple of hours, or maybe Saturdays and Sundays are your sewing days. For some people, the amount of time they have to sew changes from week to week. Whatever your schedule, make a note of your dedicated sewing time below. (Sometimes life gets in the way, and that's OK. But it really does help to know at the beginning of each week when you might be able to prioritize time for sewing.) Once you've identified them, make a note of these sewing times on your monthly calendar pages.

FINALLY, make sure to write your "Bucket List" Projects, starting on page 16. These projects can be moved to either the "Current Works-in-Progress" pages or "Long-Term Works-in-Progress" pages when you're ready to begin working on them.

Systems for Long-Term Works-in-Progress

Long-term works-in-progress are a different game altogether. For me, these are projects I don't intend to finish in a month or sometimes even in a year. I do like to dedicate regular time to working on these items, though. Think about setting aside dedicated time for them. (I plan one Saturday a month for sewing long-term works-in-progress.) Once you determine what works best for you, fill it in on page 23, and then make sure to pencil it in on your monthly calendar pages as well.

MY PLAN FOR CURRENT WORKS-IN-PROGRESS

Project: _____

Next Step: _____ ☐

Project: _____

Next Step: _____ ☐

Project: _____

Next Step: _____ ☐

Project: _____

Next Step: _____ ☐

Project: _____

Next Step: _____ ☐

Project: _____

Next Step: _____ ☐

Project: _____

Next Step: _____ ☐

Project: _____

Next Step: _____ ☐

Project: _____

Next Step: _____ ☐

Project: _____

Next Step: _____ ☐

Project: _____

Next Step: _____ ☐

Project: _____

Next Step: _____ ☐

Project: _____

Next Step: _____ ☐

Project: _____

Next Step: _____ ☐

Project: _____

Next Step: _____ ☐

Project: _____

Next Step: _____ ☐

MY PLAN FOR LONG-TERM WORKS-IN-PROGRESS

Long-Term Project: _____

Next Step: _____ ☐

Next Step: _____ ☐

Long-Term Project: _____

Next Step: _____ ☐

Next Step: _____ ☐

Long-Term Project: _____

Next Step: _____ ☐

Next Step: _____ ☐

Long-Term Project: _____

Next Step: _____ ☐

Next Step: _____ ☐

Long-Term Project: _____

Next Step: _____ ☐

Next Step: _____ ☐

Long-Term Project: _____

Next Step: _____ ☐

Next Step: _____ ☐

Long-Term Project: _____

Next Step: _____ ☐

Next Step: _____ ☐

Long-Term Project: _____

Next Step: _____ ☐

Next Step: _____ ☐

Block-of-the-Month & Sew-Along Projects

Use this space to record your block-of-the-month and sew-along projects. With so many of these weekly and monthly projects available it can be a bit overwhelming. Dedicate a few hours one day a month for keeping up with these projects. And if you fall behind, focus on one project before worrying about others you may have going on. It's OK to set some of these aside for the time being. Just be sure to download any patterns you might need and file them for when you are able to get back to work!

MY PLAN FOR BLOCK-OF-THE-MONTH AND SEW-ALONG PROJECTS

BOM or Sew-Along Project: _____

Scheduled on Monthly Calendar(s): ☐

BOM or Sew-Along Project: _____

Scheduled on Monthly Calendar(s): ☐

BOM or Sew-Along Project: _____

Scheduled on Monthly Calendar(s): ☐

BOM or Sew-Along Project: _____

Scheduled on Monthly Calendar(s): ☐

BOM or Sew-Along Project: _____

Scheduled on Monthly Calendar(s): ☐

BOM or Sew-Along Project: _____

Scheduled on Monthly Calendar(s): ☐

BOM or Sew-Along Project: _____

Scheduled on Monthly Calendar(s): ☐

BOM or Sew-Along Project: _____

Scheduled on Monthly Calendar(s): ☐

Systems for Sewing Room Cleaning & Organization

Plan to work on sewing room organization monthly or at least every other month. It took me many years to realize I needed to make this an ongoing task to keep my sewing space from getting out of control.

While you will find more information on this subject on page 52, here are some extra helps for this project:

» Consider moving everything out of the space (except furniture pieces unless you're planning to rearrange the space) so you can start with a blank slate. With everything removed, group similar items by category: fabrics, notions, patterns, scissors, threads, etc. Grouping like items will make it easier to put things back in your space.

» Return your most-used items into your sewing room first and place them where they are easily accessible. A frequently used ruler shouldn't be in a box, in a closet, or in a drawer under some fabric.

» Bring in often-used items next. If there's a chance you'll forget where you placed these items, record where they're stored. There are lots of places in your planner to record storage locations for seldom-used items.

» Rarely used items you wish to keep are best stored in a closet or out-of-the-way storage location. Again, be sure to record where you've put each item so you can locate them when needed.

» Lastly, donate any items that don't fit in the above categories.

ORGANIZATION GOALS

Setting organization goals related to quilting will help you keep on track. Rotate through the list of goals throughout the year, adding them to your monthly goal lists as often as needed. Some goals might include sorting threads, keeping an ongoing list of things you've run out of or need to order soon, straightening bins and items on shelves, clearing tabletop surfaces, organizing patterns and books, or cleaning out fabric bins. You know best what areas of your sewing space or supplies are the quickest to get messy or disorganized. You also know what makes you feel best when things are in order. Those are the areas around which you should set your goals. Consider also adding a note for yourself about how often you'll target each of these areas—weekly, monthly, quarterly, or annually.

GET ORGANIZED

THE AREAS I WANT TO GET (AND KEEP) ORGANIZED INCLUDE:

1. _____

2. _____

3. _____

4. _____

5. _____

6. _____

7. _____

8. _____

9. _____

10. _____

11. _____

12. _____

☐ Works-in-Progress ☐ Long-Term Projects
☐ Organization ☐ ☐

_____
month

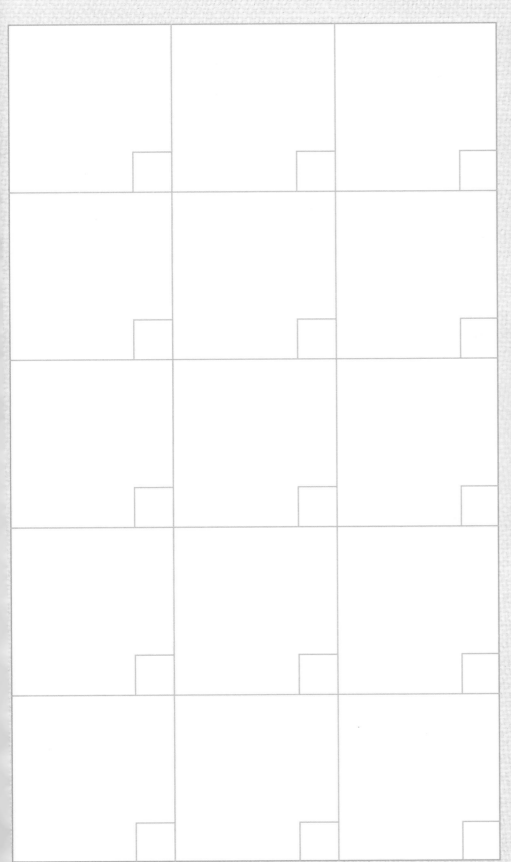

PLAN ON IT

Planners and planning systems don't have to be intimidating. Knowledge about planning basics can help you decide upon and craft an effective, workable system for yourself. The answers you wrote to the reflection questions (pages 10–13) will guide you as you begin to use this planner.

The next few pages are geared specifically toward planning for sewing and quilting (although you could plan home-related tasks at the same time). Information on planning for other home-organizing systems begins on page 77.

Planning Basics

Start developing your planning system by completing the following three steps, in order.

1. COMMIT TO PLANNING TIME

Perhaps the most important step in implementing a planning system is to choose a regular time for review, goal setting, and scheduling. (It wasn't until I routinely made this a part of my week that I really began to see consistent progress and bigger results.) Set an appointment with yourself each week to develop your planning skills. The time you spend planning is minimal compared to the time you'll end up saving and using more effectively. Commit to the time you'll spend planning and record it below before moving on.

MY DEDICATED TIME FOR SEWING AND QUILTING PLANNING/REVIEW IS:

2. FILL OUT THE MONTHLY, QUARTERLY, AND PROJECT PLANNING PAGES AS NEEDED

Capturing your plans in writing will ensure that you have all the information you need when you hold your quilting planning and review sessions. Refer back to these pages often to review and update them.

MONTHLY TOP THREE GOALS

Success in meeting goals is often the result of focus. To avoid overcommitting or overwhelming yourself, limit the number of goals you set. Try to set three (and only three) quilting-related goals for yourself just before the start of each month. Write them down on page 30. Then you'll be able to refer to these goals when you begin your planning sessions. (Overachievers and list lovers—weekly and daily "Top Three" lists may also be helpful). Set your sights to succeed!

MONTHLY PLANNING PAGES

There are 12 undated monthly calendars, such as the one on pages 32 and 33. As you fill in the dates and appointment information, block out time for sewing and organizational tasks using the tips and techniques shared throughout the planner.

QUARTERLY REVIEWS

The "Quarterly Reviews" are on page 66. Write your list of ideas at the beginning of each quarter. Having this list readily available really helps with monthly and weekly planning. And if you don't finish one of your goals, you can easily move it to the next quarter.

PROJECT PLANNING PAGES

Along with listing your current, long-term, and bucket list projects (see pages 16–19), you may wish to have more complete information for many projects. For these types of projects, use the "Project Planner" pages beginning on page 81. Use the space to include those things you need to remember, including supplies, specific next steps, and project notes.

3. UTILIZE AN AGENDA

Meetings are often a waste of time if there isn't an agenda available. Think of an agenda as a road map for where you hope to head. Use the sample five-step agenda below (or craft your own related to your current circumstances). This process should go smoothly *IF* you've entered your thoughts in the "Monthly Planners," "Monthly Top Three Goals" (page 30), "Quarterly Reviews" (page 66), and project planning lists (pages 16–18).

1. **Take a few minutes to reflect** on the past month (or week) using the reflection section questions and ideas on pages 10–13 to guide your thoughts.

2. **Go through the review process** outlined on pages 64–67.

3. **Update your calendar** with any appointments, meetings, or events you're attending, such as a guild meeting, a quilting class, or a consultation with your professional quilter.

4. **Plan your sewing time.** Schedule time to quilt on your calendar; note the beginning and ending time for sewing sessions. Consider scheduling an extra session as a cushion in case you miss one.

5. **Schedule time for sewing room organization, scrap management, and other sewing-related tasks,** separate from your sewing time.

MORE TIPS FOR PLANNING

If you're having a hard time getting out of the starting gate when it comes to planning, try these ideas.

» Write all over the planner pages; don't be afraid to use them and adjust your plans as you go. Put the pages to work for you!

» Look over your "Monthly Top Three Goals" (page 30) and the projects/patterns you've included there. Can you set some monthly or weekly goals—a number of blocks to sew, a section of appliqué to complete, or a couple of hours to do a fabric pull?

» Turn to "Long-Term Works-in-Progress" (page 18) and write in a few steps that will help you move one project forward.

» On your "Current Works-in-Progress" list (page 16) add deadlines for must-finish items that have a definite due date (such as a baby shower gift), then break down the project into achievable segments, such as so many blocks per week, or time to quilt or bind it, etc.

» Pencil in an upcoming retreat or sewing event and plan time to prep a project and pack ahead of the event so you leave with everything you need.

UNLESS COMMITMENT
IS MADE, THERE ARE
ONLY PROMISES
AND HOPES . . . BUT
NO PLANS.
—PETER F. DRUCKER

Monthly Top Three Goals

One key to effective goal setting is limiting the number of goals you set. Doing so allows you to focus on what is MOST important and can help avoid overwhelming you with an unachievable list.

MONTH _____

1. _____

2. _____

3. _____

MONTH _____

1. _____

2. _____

3. _____

MONTH _____

1. _____

2. _____

3. _____

MONTH _____

1. _____

2. _____

3. _____

IF YOU DON'T KNOW WHERE YOU'RE GOING,
YOU'LL WIND UP SOMEWHERE ELSE.
—YOGI BERRA

MONTH _____

1. _____

2. _____

3. _____

MONTH _____

1. _____

2. _____

3. _____

MONTH _____

1. _____

2. _____

3. _____

MONTH _____

1. _____

2. _____

3. _____

MONTH _____

1. _____

2. _____

3. _____

MONTH _____

1. _____

2. _____

3. _____

MONTH _____

1. _____

2. _____

3. _____

MONTH _____

1. _____

2. _____

3. _____

REVIEW YOUR GOALS AND SCHEDULE TIME FOR:

☐ Works-in-Progress ☐ Long-Term Projects
☐ Organization ☐ ☐

month

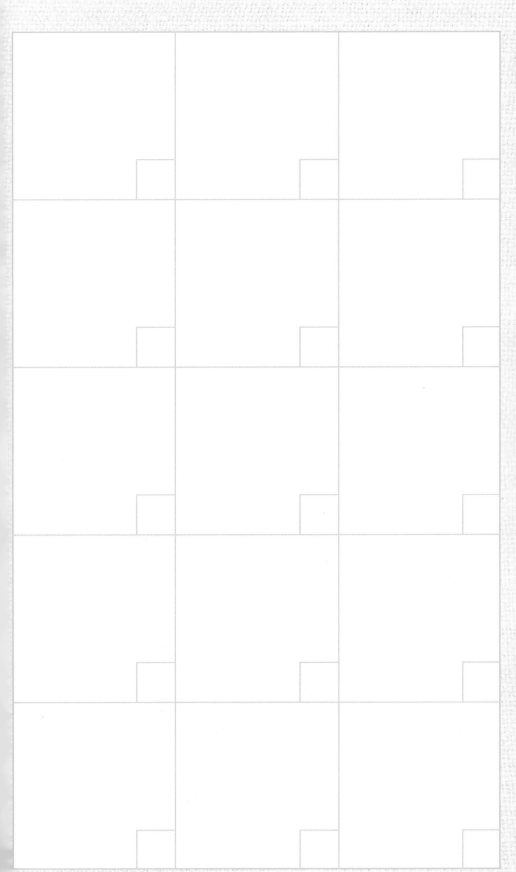

FABRIC & SCRAP MANAGEMENT

When it comes to favorite supplies, it's a safe bet that FABRIC tops the list for many (if not all) quilters. Knowing what you have and where it is will inevitably allow more time to do what you love most—QUILT! So let's plan for order and organization when it comes to keeping track of larger cuts of fabric, precuts, and scraps.

Later, you'll do an inventory of your patterns, books, rulers, and notions (pages 42–46) to help you save time looking for something you know you have somewhere.

For now, turn the page for tips and tricks to help you keep an inventory and organize the fabrics you have on hand.

Systems for Stash Management

Most quilters quickly discover that their fabric stash seems to mysteriously multiply. When precuts, scraps, and yardage purchases aren't tended to regularly, they can grow out of control. Save time in looking for fabrics by having a system for taking care of your stash and using the fabrics you have. The topic of scrap management is covered in a separate section on page 38 to make managing them a bit easier. And, notions, tools, and patterns also have their own sections beginning on page 42. But you'll definitely want to inventory your precuts (you can also list any coordinating fabric you might have with those), large cuts for borders, bindings, and backings, and background fabrics. Personally, I don't include fat quarters in these inventories because I organize them by color. Here, I just focus on larger pieces that are useful to know where they are and how much I have on hand.

MY PLAN FOR STASH MANAGEMENT

A GOOD SYSTEM SHORTENS THE ROAD TO THE GOAL.
—ORISON SWETT MARDEN

Large Cuts Fabric Inventory

While it's virtually impossible to document every piece of fabric in your stash (unless you're a very minimalist quilter), it is helpful to keep track of the variety of fabrics you have on hand. If you like to purchase your favorite background fabrics in bulk so that you're always stocked up, make sure you keep a list of them. If you purchase 1 yard or more of fabrics you think will make great borders, bindings, or both, you'll likewise want to write them on your list. And what quilter doesn't love a good sale for purchasing quilt backing? It's nice to have an inventory of the larger cuts of fabric you own so that when the time comes to piece a quilt back, you know just what choices you have on hand.

FABRIC FOR: _____   FABRIC FOR: _____

YARDAGE: _____   YARDAGE: _____

LOCATION: _____   LOCATION: _____

FABRIC FOR: _____   FABRIC FOR: _____

YARDAGE: _____   YARDAGE: _____

LOCATION: _____   LOCATION: _____

FABRIC FOR: _____   FABRIC FOR: _____

YARDAGE: _____   YARDAGE: _____

LOCATION: _____   LOCATION: _____

FABRIC FOR: _____   FABRIC FOR: _____

YARDAGE: _____   YARDAGE: _____

LOCATION: _____   LOCATION: _____

FABRIC FOR: _____   FABRIC FOR: _____

YARDAGE: _____   YARDAGE: _____

LOCATION: _____   LOCATION: _____

FABRIC FOR: _____   FABRIC FOR: _____

YARDAGE: _____   YARDAGE: _____

LOCATION: _____   LOCATION: _____

FABRIC FOR: _____   FABRIC FOR: _____

YARDAGE: _____   YARDAGE: _____

LOCATION: _____   LOCATION: _____

FABRIC FOR: _____   FABRIC FOR: _____

YARDAGE: _____   YARDAGE: _____

LOCATION: _____   LOCATION: _____

Inventory of Precuts

Precuts can be a quilter's best friend. Whether you're tempted by a particular designer's collections or you just want a piece of every fabric in a collection, precuts are a quick way to have it all! They can also sometimes be an impulse grab-and-go purchase without a pattern in mind. But don't let your precuts languish. Keep a list of what you have. Then when the perfect pattern calling for precuts comes along, you'll be sitting pretty with a list from which to peruse and choose!

Listed below are the Moda Fabrics precut sizes (other manufacturers vary in the number of pieces included their bundles).

» Mini Charm Packs: 42 squares, 2½" × 2½"

» Charm Packs: 42 squares, 5" × 5"

» Honey Buns: 40 strips, 1½" × 42"

» Jelly Rolls: 40 strips, 2½" × 42"

» Layer Cakes: 42 squares, 10" × 10"

» Fat-Eighth Bundle (one piece, 9" × 21", of each print in a collection—number of pieces may vary).

» Fat-Quarter Bundle (one piece, 18" × 21", of each print in a collection—number of pieces may vary).

PRECUT SIZE/TYPE: _____

I HAVE: _____

_____

_____

_____

_____

_____

PRECUT SIZE/TYPE: _____

I HAVE: _____

_____

_____

_____

_____

_____

PRECUT SIZE/TYPE: _____

I HAVE: _____

_____

_____

_____

_____

_____

PRECUT SIZE/TYPE: _____

I HAVE: _____

_____

_____

_____

_____

_____

PRECUT SIZE/TYPE: _____

I HAVE: _____
_____
_____
_____
_____
_____
_____
_____

PRECUT SIZE/TYPE: _____

I HAVE: _____
_____
_____
_____
_____
_____
_____
_____

PRECUT SIZE/TYPE: _____

I HAVE: _____
_____
_____
_____
_____
_____
_____
_____

PRECUT SIZE/TYPE: _____

I HAVE: _____
_____
_____
_____
_____
_____
_____
_____

PRECUT SIZE/TYPE: _____

I HAVE: _____
_____
_____
_____
_____
_____
_____
_____

PRECUT SIZE/TYPE: _____

I HAVE: _____
_____
_____
_____
_____
_____
_____
_____

PRECUT SIZE/TYPE: _____

I HAVE: _____
_____
_____
_____
_____
_____
_____
_____

PRECUT SIZE/TYPE: _____

I HAVE: _____
_____
_____
_____
_____
_____
_____
_____

Systems for Scraps

If you're a scrap saver, taking time to take charge of your scraps will be a time-saver in the end. By creating a system to work exclusively on scraps for a couple of hours one day a month, you'll be able to make significant progress.

Keep fabrics from one collection or project together until the project is complete. Once finished, cut leftover fabric into the following sizes (based on your preferences for future projects), sorting them into bins by size:

» Fat quarters (18" × 21")

» Fat eighths (9" × 21")

» Strips: 5", 2½", and 1½" wide

» Squares: 5", 3", 2½", and 2"

» Half-square-triangle units: 2½" units
(I like to make few half-square triangles from leftover fabrics for use in later projects. It's like having a starter kit at the ready for a future scrap quilt.)

Here are a couple of other tips I use for scrap management:

» Cut up scraps while cutting out a project. Of course, you can leave bigger pieces intact in case you make a mistake and need some backup fabric. But try to cut small pieces into squares and strips as you can while working. Doing so can save so much time later and prevent fabric waste.

» Designate a scrap bin and then sort through the bin monthly. Donate scraps you know you're not likely to use and cut up and store the ones you want to keep. Sorting through this bin monthly helps to keep it from overflowing.

Use the next few pages to write down your plans. As the saying goes, "Ink it, don't just think it." Taking the time to write out your plan will give you a place to refer to when you're ready to get serious about scrap management. Breaking the job into manageable segments will help you begin getting (and staying) organized.

MY PLAN FOR SCRAP MANAGEMENT

I PLAN TO CUT MY SCRAPS INTO THESE SIZES:

☐ _____

☐ _____

☐ _____

☐ _____

☐ _____

☐ _____

☐ _____

HERE'S HOW I'M GOING TO ORGANIZE AND STORE MY SCRAPS:

_____

_____

_____

_____

_____

_____

_____

_____

_____

_____

I'M GOING TO DEVOTE TIME TO CONTROLLING MY SCRAPS:

☐ weekly   ☐ monthly   ☐ quarterly

SCRAP MANAGEMENT PROGRESS CHART

Seeing progress is believing! Record your success in controlling your scraps
and you'll be thrilled to see just how much you've done in a year!

DATE	RESULTS	DATE	RESULTS

REVIEW YOUR GOALS AND SCHEDULE TIME FOR: «««

☐ Works-in-Progress ☐ Long-Term Projects
☐ Organization ☐   ☐

month

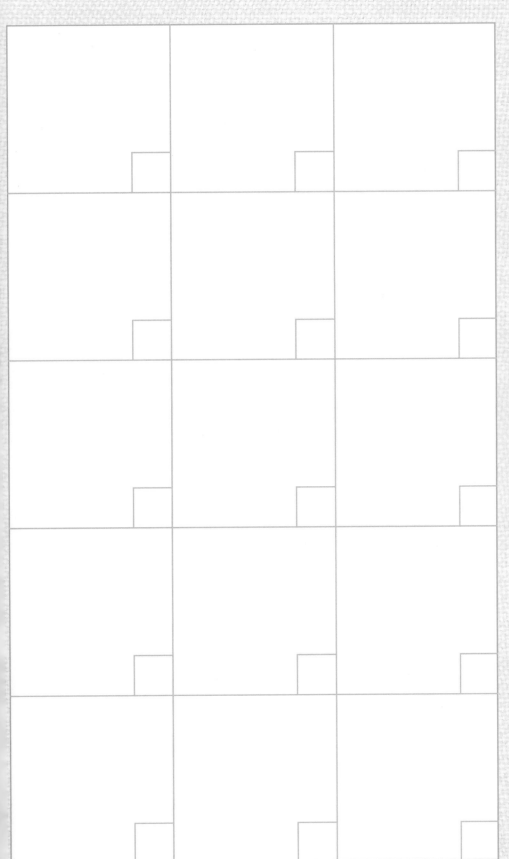

TAKING STOCK

Living in a rural area as a young mom made it necessary to do bulk shopping trips in town just once or twice a month. That taught me the importance of inventory to make sure I had what I needed and to prevent duplicate purchases.

The same holds true about keeping an inventory of sewing and quilting supplies. Taking an inventory can be very helpful as you may find patterns, tools, and notions you've previously purchased in duplicate (and even triplicate!).

Use the inventory lists that follow to keep track of and contain your patterns, rulers, specialty tools, and notions. There's also a "Wish List" on page 49 to record items you want to purchase and a "Shopping List" to keep track of items you need right away. An inventory for larger cuts of fabrics, precuts, and scraps begins on page 35.

Pattern Inventory

Sometimes you find a must-make pattern in a book or magazine. Other times you plan to make a single pattern in a plastic zip bag you purchased at your local quilt shop. Or it might be that you downloaded a PDF pattern you've purchased online.

You recall the pattern, but have you ever wondered where you put it or which book the pattern was in? Wonder no more! Use this handy checklist to write the name and location of the must-make patterns on your to-do list. You'll know exactly where to find the patterns when you're ready to make them!

PATTERN NAME   LOCATION OF PATTERN

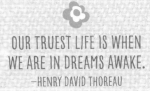

OUR TRUEST LIFE IS WHEN
WE ARE IN DREAMS AWAKE.
—HENRY DAVID THOREAU

PATTERN NAME

LOCATION OF PATTERN

Ruler Inventory

Sometimes it seems as if there are more rulers on the market than one could ever figure out how to use. Much like having the right tool for a home remodeling project, many designers have a favorite ruler that makes cutting out a pattern or assembling a block easier. When you're getting ready to begin a new project, refer to this at-a-glance inventory to know what rulers you have on hand and which ones you need. In the long run, if you keep the list updated, the inventory will help avoid duplication and also help you know where to locate those rulers in your sewing space.

The lists are divided into three categories: "Standard Rulers," "Utility Rulers," and "Specialty Rulers." The section headings for each list give a basic definition of these different classifications.

STANDARD RULERS

Standard rulers are the sizes commonly used for cutting, such as 6" × 12", 8½" × 24", and 12½" square.

HAVE	NEED	SIZE OR SHAPE AND BRAND	LOCATION
☐	☐		
☐	☐		
☐	☐		
☐	☐		
☐	☐		
☐	☐		
☐	☐		
☐	☐		
☐	☐		
☐	☐		

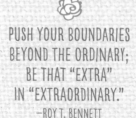

PUSH YOUR BOUNDARIES
BEYOND THE ORDINARY;
BE THAT "EXTRA"
IN "EXTRAORDINARY."
—ROY T. BENNETT

UTILITY RULERS

Utility rulers are additional sizes of square rulers that can be used for squaring up blocks, or specific-function rulers such as a Bloc Loc or Simple Folded Corners Ruler.

HAVE	NEED	SIZE OR SHAPE AND BRAND	LOCATION
☐	☐		
☐	☐		
☐	☐		
☐	☐		
☐	☐		
☐	☐		
☐	☐		
☐	☐		
☐	☐		
☐	☐		

SPECIALTY RULERS

Specialty rulers are those with a very specific use such as for cutting or trimming Log Cabins, Pineapples, or Hexagons.

HAVE	NEED	SIZE OR SHAPE AND BRAND	LOCATION
☐	☐		
☐	☐		
☐	☐		
☐	☐		
☐	☐		
☐	☐		
☐	☐		
☐	☐		
☐	☐		
☐	☐		

Specialty Tools & Notions Inventory

Unless you've been good about culling your supplies over the years, the list of little extras you buy and forget you have might be long. These little add-ons add up in terms of money spent and the space they take up in your sewing room. Write them in your planner to eliminate the game of chance, wondering whether or not you already have certain items. Fusible interfacing, diagonal seam tape, zippers, triangle-square papers in assorted sizes, invisible thread—list them here. When you're making a shopping list for your next project, refer to this list to see what you have and what you need. It's also a handy reference when there's a stock-up sale at your favorite quilt shop. But remember, don't just stock and stash those specialty tools and notions. Add them to your list.

TOOLS & NOTIONS

HAVE	NEED	SIZE OR SHAPE AND BRAND	LOCATION
☐	☐		
☐	☐		
☐	☐		
☐	☐		
☐	☐		
☐	☐		
☐	☐		
☐	☐		
☐	☐		
☐	☐		
☐	☐		
☐	☐		
☐	☐		
☐	☐		
☐	☐		
☐	☐		
☐	☐		
☐	☐		

Shopping List

Eliminate the guesswork so you'll be sure to have what you need when you're ready to sew. As you use up supplies, write down the items you need to replenish. Check off what you purchase and add additional items to the list as necessary. You'll be happy to have the list the next time you're at the quilt shop and asking yourself, "Now what was it I needed to pick up?"

MAY THE SUN SHINE ALL DAY LONG,
EVERYTHING GO RIGHT AND
NOTHING WRONG. MAY THOSE
YOU LOVE BRING LOVE BACK TO YOU,
AND MAY ALL THE WISHES
YOU WISH COME TRUE.
—IRISH BLESSING

Wish List

Make a list of items that you'd like to have, but are willing to wait to purchase until you know more, find a good deal, or both. You may wish to add a reference as to the project/pattern you'll use this item with. This is also a great list to refer to when your family or friends ask you for gift ideas.

☐
☐
☐
☐
☐
☐
☐
☐
☐
☐
☐
☐
☐
☐
☐
☐
☐
☐
☐
☐
☐
☐
☐
☐
☐
☐
☐
☐
☐
☐

☐
☐
☐
☐
☐
☐
☐
☐
☐
☐
☐
☐
☐
☐
☐
☐
☐
☐
☐
☐
☐
☐
☐
☐
☐
☐
☐
☐
☐

REVIEW YOUR GOALS AND SCHEDULE TIME FOR:

☐ Works-in-Progress ☐ Long-Term Projects

☐ Organization ☐ _____ ☐ _____

month

GET ORGANIZED!

An organized sewing space can be not only a thing of beauty but also a means of freeing up more time to sew. Save time by not hunting for things you need! There are many different approaches to organizing your sewing space. Often, a clean start is the best way to go. Removing absolutely every item except the furniture pieces from the space before beginning can help you recognize how many items you have that you might not want to put back. But for some, this method seems overwhelming. Never fear. There are options! Choose the method that works best for you. Ahead, you'll find helpful hints for beginning the process.

20 Steps to an Organized Sewing Space

BEFORE YOU BEGIN

» Brainstorm about your space and how you want it to function. Prioritize which areas to focus on first. (You don't have to use the suggested order.)

» Break up projects into smaller steps if needed.

» Make a time estimate for each step and put it on a calendar. Or choose one day each week to tackle one of these projects.

HELPFUL HINTS

» Be realistic. An organized sewing space won't be finished overnight!

» Batch similar tasks. For instance, you might want to tackle books, patterns, and magazines in one sitting, and focus on rulers during another time slot if you have a lot of specialty rulers.

» Use "time blocking." Time blocking means that you set aside a certain amount of time for a task on a given day. Turn off your phone and try for minimal interruptions and distractions during this time period.

» When you plan, add 50% extra time to your estimate. This will help make sure you stay on schedule.

» Start with the easiest thing on your list so you can gain momentum.

» Be willing to adjust your timetable as needed. Remember that you want to keep sewing too.

STEPS TO AN ORGANIZED SEWING SPACE

☐ 1. Take a "before" picture.

☐ 2. Make a list of works in progress.

☐ 3. Start a "to make" list (you'll add to this as you move through the organizing process).

☐ 4. Clear off flat surfaces (don't forget the sewing table, ironing board, cutting area, and any shelves in your space).

☐ 5. Gather all of your rulers, rotary cutters, and scissors, and assign them a home.

☐ 6. Organize thread and bobbins.

☐ 7. Organize other miscellaneous notions.

☐ 8. Remove all fabric and gather it in one space (use a dining room table, the top of a bed, plastic storage boxes, etc.).

☐ 9. Decide which fabric to keep and which to donate or sell.

☐ 10. Choose a method for storing and organizing scraps.

☐ 11. Divide quilting books into three piles: keep, organize, and donate.

☐ 12. Divide quilting patterns into three piles: keep, organize, and donate.

☐ 13. Divide magazines into three piles: keep, organize, and donate. If you are only keeping a magazine for one or two patterns, remove and place them in sheet protectors in a three-ring binder. (Make sure that you have all the pages needed; sometimes patterns are continued on later pages or on a pullout pattern sheet.)

☐ 14. Plan your storage. Measure your spaces before doing any shopping. Look for containers at The Container Store, Target, Walmart, and Dollar Stores.

☐ 15. Make a shopping list.

☐ 16. Shop for the items on your list.

☐ 17. Organize everything with your new containers.

☐ 18. Take an "after" photo!

☐ 19. Make sure you've given away the donation fabrics, patterns, and notions and listed the "to sell" items.

☐ 20. Enjoy your organized space. Review your to-do list and start quilting!

Organization Goals

Say it, forget it. Write it, remember it. That's an adage that many of us can relate to. Writing down your quilt-related organization goals will not only help you to plan how to meet them but also enable you to prioritize the ones that are most important to you. Rotate these goals on your monthly planners, including them as often as needed to meet your objectives. What kinds of goals might you include? Consider these: straightening bins and shelves, clearing tabletop surfaces, organizing patterns and books, sorting threads, or cleaning out fabric bins. You're the best judge of which areas are the quickest to get out of control in your sewing space. Those are the areas around which you should set your goals. Consider noting for yourself how often you'll target each of these areas—weekly, monthly, quarterly, or annually. Doing so can help you stay on track.

MY GOALS

The areas I want to get (and keep) organized include:

1.

2.

3.

4.

5.

6.

7.

8.

9.

10.

11.

Simplify Your Storage

An organized sewing space is an efficient sewing space. The role that storage plays in organization is key. Good storage is essential, but it needn't be expensive (for years I kept projects in pizza boxes while I collected other bins and boxes for project storage). I recommend waiting to purchase storage items until you've first used items you have readily available and you've worked through some basic organization and made a list of what you might need. Here are a few of my favorite storage solutions:

» Consider using baskets and open bins instead of covered plastic bins so that air can circulate around your fabrics and projects.

» Labels provide an at-a-glance way to keep items organized and easy to find, particularly if your bins are not transparent. Labels don't have to be fancy. Find a labeling system that works for you and use it consistently. I use a combination of adhesive labels I write on and bin clips from The Container Store. The labels are easy to change when the contents of the bin or basket changes.

» Store like items together. Your most-used tools should be within arm's reach of your sewing machine or cutting table (depending on how you use them). Items used less frequently might be stored in a cupboard or closet. As much as possible, store similar items in one location. For example, store your rulers in one spot, not three different places around the room.

» Pretty dishes and bowls are cute and clever ways to store sewing notions and small items. Glass mason jars are another favorite way to corral small items in see-through style.

START BY DOING WHAT'S NECESSARY; THEN DO WHAT'S POSSIBLE; AND SUDDENLY YOU ARE DOING THE IMPOSSIBLE.
—FRANCIS OF ASSISI

HELPFUL HINTS

1. Make sure your most-used items are readily available and easily accessible to where you most use them. Place frequently used rulers in a bin on your cutting area, sprays and starches near the ironing board, and a pair of scissors and a seam ripper near the sewing machine.

2. Less frequently used items can be placed in drawers or bins where they are still easy to access but out of the way and not mistaken for clutter.

3. Items used occasionally can be stored in a closet, drawer, or box—just make sure to record where these items are.

4. Donate or sell items that you haven't used or no longer plan to use.

My Storage Wish List

Jot down your storage needs below, including dimensions of shelves. (Knowing the height, width, and depth will be handy when you're looking for what fits your space best.) You might also keep track of specific bin and basket sizes and/or brands you purchase in case you need more or are waiting for a sale!

1.

2.

3.

4.

5.

6.

7.

8.

REVIEW YOUR GOALS AND SCHEDULE TIME FOR:
☐ Works-in-Progress ☐ Long-Term Projects
☐ Organization ☐   ☐

_____
month

WHAT & WHERE

If you frequently freshen up your home by changing quilts, pillows, runners, and other quilted decor items, keeping a list of what you've made and where you store those items can help them from falling out of sight and out of mind. It's also handy to include where you most frequently display the pieces. When it's time to plan for a new decor item, refer to this list to determine areas you don't yet have a plan for or to recall an area you're looking to update.

Seasonal Quilts & Decor Items Inventory

Keep track of your cherished holiday or seasonal quilts, pillows, runners, wall hangings, and more.

DECOR ITEM	STORAGE LOCATION	PLACEMENT

I DON'T KNOW WHAT LIES AROUND THE BEND, BUT I'M
GOING TO BELIEVE THAT THE BEST DOES . —L.M. MONTGOMERY

DECOR ITEM	STORAGE LOCATION	PLACEMENT

continued from page 59

DECOR ITEM	STORAGE LOCATION	PLACEMENT

Home Decor Project Ideas

Use the following space to record those ideas that come to mind about future decor projects you want to make. Be intentional here about what you want and need. Walk around your home and note places where you might want to create something to use for decoration. Measure the wall space, table space, or pillow size you want for each of these projects, and record your information, placement area, and project pattern ideas in the appropriate columns below.

DECOR IDEA	PLACEMENT	PATTERN & MEASUREMENTS

REVIEW YOUR GOALS AND SCHEDULE TIME FOR:

☐ Works-in-Progress ☐ Long-Term Projects
☐ Organization ☐

month

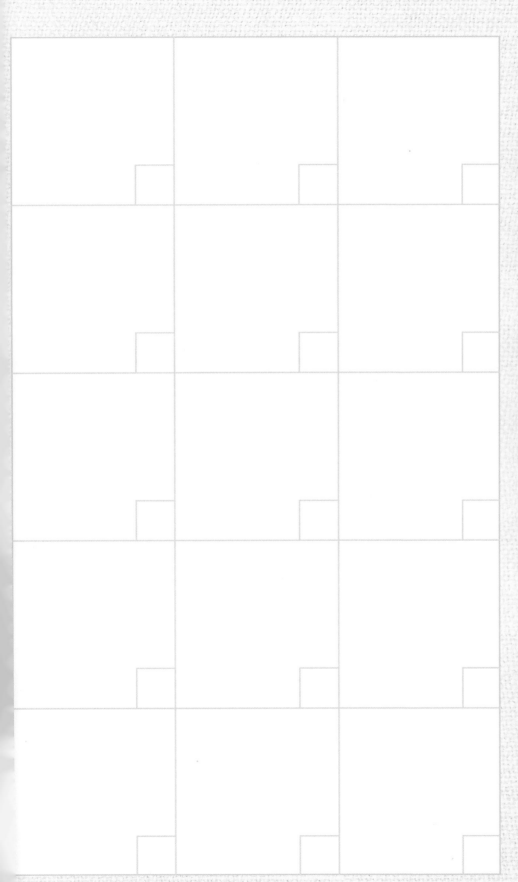

REVIEW REGULARLY

The process and importance of regular review is something that many people don't take advantage of fully. While lots of quilters record things fairly regularly in a variety of notebooks and journals, many don't to go back to those notes in order to help projects stay on track. This often leads to forgetting things you've spent a fair amount of time thinking about already and duplicating those efforts later. Falling behind on goals you've set for yourself is also a by-product of not reviewing regularly. Likewise, without review, you're unable to see (and celebrate!) your progress along the way.

You'll be amazed at how regular check-ins (weekly, monthly, quarterly, and annually) help keep you on track. Turn the page for more ideas!

How Often Should I Review?

Embrace review as a major component of keeping up and staying organized. If you're keen on making review an integral part of your life overall, consider scheduling a weekly, monthly, quarterly, and yearly review for both your home and work projects. And separately review your sewing and quilting at similar intervals. Think about how much time you're able to dedicate to quilting. If you sew regularly, you'll likely need to review more often. An avid quilter might schedule weekly or monthly review sessions. If you sew less frequently, a quarterly review could be regular enough to keep on track. Consider the following during your review process.

REVIEW TASKS

Step through this process as you conduct your reviews:

1. Read quickly or skim through your *A Quilting Life Planner and Workbook*—yes, flip through all of the pages where you've recorded goals. (Try placing an adhesive tab at the top of every page you regularly revisit.)

2. Make written notes of the items you marked for review. Writing things down will help them stick in your memory better than a mental checklist does.

3. If you've finished any projects, mark them as completed and add any notes.

4. Make a list of things you've accomplished or done well.

5. Once that recap is complete, make a list of projects or areas to focus on for the coming time period (weekly, monthly, or quarterly), depending on how often you've decided to review.

Use this and pages 65 and 66 to make notes as you review.

TIPS FOR WEEKLY, MONTHLY, AND YEARLY REVIEWS

» A weekly review shouldn't take too long. In just a few minutes, review what you've accomplished for the week and make a few notes or plans for the coming week.

» Invest about 30 minutes in a monthly review. Being more thorough than you are with a weekly review will allow time to go over the systems you're using and determine how they are working for you, along with your project progress.

» For a quarterly or yearly review, go through all of the steps outlined in the "Review Tasks" section above.

MY REVIEW PLAN

BE KIND TO YOURSELF

The mantra "progress, not perfection" is definitely one to keep in mind as you navigate living your best quilting life. It will take some time and practice to make the review process a regular part of your sewing and quilting. In fact, for most people it takes a long time to learn this process (I feel like I'm still learning too). So, remember to go easy on yourself. Getting and staying organized, like anything else, is truly a journey.

TO STAY ON TRACK, TAKING THE TIME
TO REVISE & UPDATE YOUR PROGRESS IS IMPORTANT.

WHAT IS WORKING WELL?

WHAT CATEGORIES/PROJECTS/AREAS SHOULD I BE GIVING EXTRA TIME TO? LESS TIME TO?
(TAKE THE TIME TO REVISE/UPDATE ANYTHING YOU'VE MADE NOTE OF HERE.)

TASK CHECKLIST
Use the table below to record any tasks you've thought to add to your to-do list as you complete your review sessions.

Task:	Task:
Finished ☐	Finished ☐
Task:	Task:
Finished ☐	Finished ☐
Task:	Task:
Finished ☐	Finished ☐
Task:	Task:
Finished ☐	Finished ☐
Task:	Task:
Finished ☐	Finished ☐

REFLECTION IS ONE OF THE MOST UNDERUSED YET POWERFUL TOOLS FOR SUCCESS.
~RICHARD CARLSON

Quarterly Reviews

QUARTER _____ / _____ / _____ _____

_____

_____

_____

_____

QUARTER _____ / _____ / _____

_____

_____

_____

_____

_____

_____

QUARTER _____ / _____ / _____ _____

_____

_____

_____

_____

_____

QUARTER _____ / _____ / _____

_____

_____

_____

_____

_____

_____

month

REVIEW YOUR GOALS AND SCHEDULE TIME FOR:

☐ Works-in-Progress ☐ Long-Term Projects
☐ Organization ☐ ☐

GIVING & GIFTING

It's easy to get overwhelmed with good intentions. And some seasons of life are better suited than others for taking on a wide range of charity sewing projects. Think about how important this type of sewing is to you and set goals that work with your life stage and your available time and resources.

As well, the idea of making handmade gifts for everyone on your gift list might sound appealing, but if you don't work on those gifts year-round, the busyness of real life gets in the way and you wish you'd started sooner. This month get more intentional about these two fun categories of sewing. By making your list and checking it twice (a month?), you'll stay on top of your heart's desires.

Sewing for Charity

Many quilters sew for charitable causes, making quilts for veterans, sewing to donate pillowcases, baby quilts, kids' quilts, and more. When you find causes that are near and dear to your heart, write down the organization's details here, including their needs, pattern recommendations, and a website where you can check for updated information.

CHARITY/CAUSE NAME

PROJECT NOTES/DETAILS

Gifts to Make

A quilt is a hug you can wrap up in. That's why many of us love to quilt for family and friends and to commemorate special occasions. Once you've found the perfect pattern for someone on your gift list, keep track of the details here. You'll be relieved to refer to this list rather than searching your memory when you're ready to begin!

FOR	OCCASION	PATTERN I PLAN TO MAKE	FINISHED
			☐
			☐
			☐
			☐
			☐
			☐
			☐
			☐
			☐
			☐
			☐
			☐
			☐
			☐
			☐
			☐
			☐
			☐
			☐
			☐
			☐
			☐

REVIEW YOUR GOALS AND SCHEDULE TIME FOR:

☐ Works-in-Progress ☐ Long-Term Projects
☐ Organization ☐ _____

_____
month

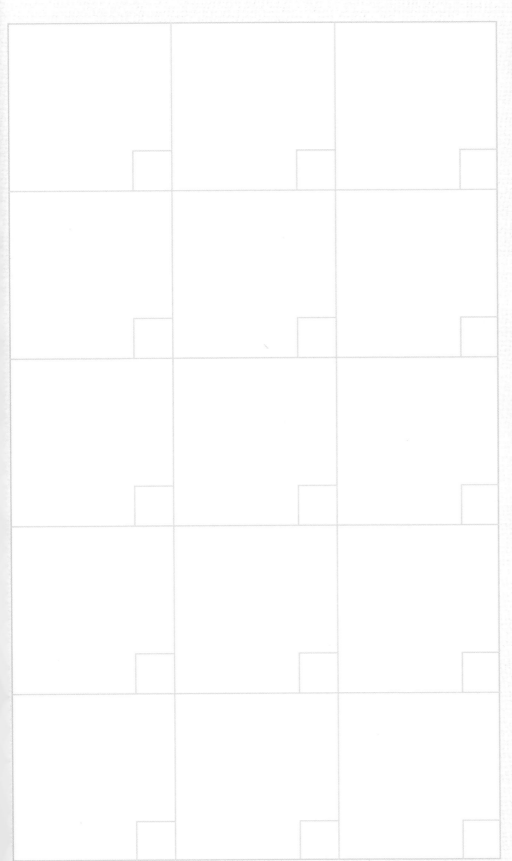

YOUR JOURNEY & LEGACY

Think about one of the very first quilts you made. Do you still have it? Is it displayed in a place of prominence or hidden out of sight? One of my favorites is an early quilt in my journey that definitely wasn't perfect, but to me it was beautiful. I hung it where I passed by it several times a day. As I became more skilled in quilting, I sometimes noticed the cut-off corners and wonky blocks as I walked by. But over the years, noticing those quirks and imperfections made the quilt all the more valuable to me. This very imperfect project came to represent my love for quilting and specifically my appreciation for my progress through quilting and through life.

Like me, you are a quilter. You are on a journey that will create a legacy of beauty, and documenting that is an important step in the process.

My Quilting Heritage & Legacy

When I teach and talk to quilters from all over the world, I learn that many are "first generation" quilters. Others are blessed, as I am, to have had a grandmother or other family member help them navigate this beautiful hobby. Still others have lifelong friends who walk alongside them on their quilting journey. Whatever your story—your heritage, your path—be sure to record your thoughts about your experiences.

MY QUILTING HERITAGE

WRITE A BIT ABOUT YOUR QUILTING HERITAGE HERE, INCLUDING YOUR OWN JOURNEY. IF YOU ARE THE FIRST PERSON TO QUILT IN YOUR FAMILY, THEN FOCUS PRIMARILY ON HOW YOU CAME TO BE A QUILTER.

THINGS I'VE LEARNED BECAUSE I AM A QUILTER

IF YOUR ACTIONS CREATE A LEGACY THAT INSPIRES OTHERS TO DREAM MORE, LEARN MORE,
DO MORE, AND BECOME MORE, THEN YOU ARE AN EXCELLENT LEADER. —DOLLY PARTON

THINGS I WANT TO BECOME A PART OF MY QUILTING LEGACY *(Use this section to record your thoughts and dreams for future quilting endeavors. This might also include how you want to possibly influence others through your quilting in your circle of friends and family.)*

REVIEW YOUR GOALS AND SCHEDULE TIME FOR:

☐ Works-in-Progress ☐ Long-Term Projects

☐ Organization ☐ ☐

month

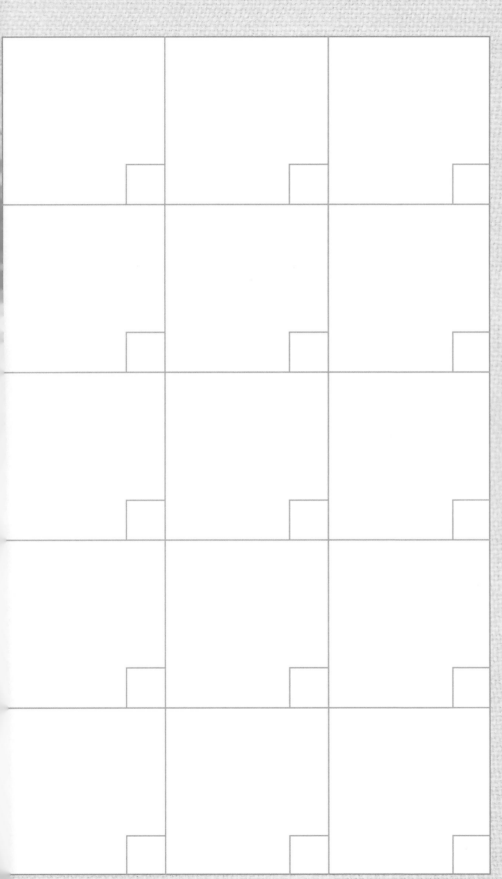

HOME ORGANIZING SYSTEMS

Having effective home organizing systems for keeping your calendar current, mail and paper handling, menu planning, and cleaning creates more time for sewing. By focusing on getting your home organizing systems in place, you can have more time for the things you want to do and for the people you love. By staying on top of your calendar, mail and paper tasks, menu planning, and cleaning, you also might be able to eliminate stress and concentrate more on what you want to spend time thinking about. If you're ready to organize outside your sewing room, read on!

Calendar Systems & Helps

1. Consider using a combination of digital and paper calendars. While you might record appointments and events on your phone's calendar, transferring them to a paper calendar at the beginning of each month gives you a visual aid to spot your busiest days and any free blocks of time.

2. Keep a perpetual birthday calendar (listing the month/day) and also transfer those to your paper calendar monthly so you don't miss a chance to send well wishes.

3. Use a magnetic calendar/dry erase board in your office and/or sewing room where you always list the "Monthly Top Three" goals (page 30). (The "Top Three" list isn't limited to quilting; consider creating a family- or work-related weekly "Top Three" goal list and posting them near an oft-used space.)

4. Review your paper calendar in each weekly planning session to prevent overlooking important upcoming events and meetings.

Systems for Handling Mail & Paper

1. Process mail daily and immediately shred or recycle everything that you don't need to keep.

2. Place everything else in a designated basket and review it all weekly. At that point, pay the bills, file items that need to be saved, and add to your calendar any invitations or other events.

3. For other mail and paper handling solutions, check out these additional resources:
   » *The Paper Solution* by Lisa Woodruff
   » "Sunday Basket" system, also by Lisa Woodruff, at organize365.com

Menu Planning

1. Menu planning is highly individualized. A mom with four young children at home might meal-plan monthly and put a lot of simple family-friendly dinners on a rotation system to simplify. An older couple without children at home may plan weekly and have a bit more flexibility with meal choices.

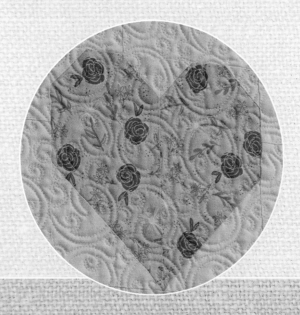

2. Kendra Adachi (author of *The Lazy Genius Way*) has a wonderful idea of having a list of "brainless crowd-please recipes." These are meals with simple, easy-to-have-on-hand ingredients that one can always make in a hurry. They are perfect for when you want to sew the day away and not worry too much about food or cooking. You'd think it would be simple to remember these types of meals, but having a list is so incredibly helpful. Start a list of your favorite meals to make in this way.

3. Keep a running shopping list. If you like to shop in a bulk warehouse store, plan a monthly visit and take your list with you to save time.

4. Take advantage of grocery delivery services to free up time spent shopping.

5. Consider using a meal box service once a month to expand your cooking horizons and mix things up. You likely won't mind spending a little time cooking if all the ingredients are just waiting to be prepared.

Cleaning Systems

1. Decide what you want to get done along with the frequency for each chore and write them down. Use this as your overall plan to guide the rest of your decisions.

2. Determine if it works better for you to do a little each day or to focus on cleaning for a larger block of time weekly or biweekly. If you're overwhelmed by the lists or you frequently run out of time to complete things, try to do at least one chore each day so that your longer weekly sessions aren't too long.

3. A little online research will yield lots of results to peruse; find a system that works for you. Over the years I've used a variety of different systems, including the Fly Lady cleaning method, the Clean Mama system, and others that I've improvised based on our home.

4. Divide and conquer. Enlist help from other members in your household, making sure the chores are divided appropriately. The old saying "many hands make light work" contains a lot of truth. Usually, everyone can end up doing more of the tasks they enjoy, keeping dreaded tasks to a minimum.

5. If you're able, consider enlisting a cleaning service on a regular or semi-regular basis to free up some time for more pressing demands on your time.

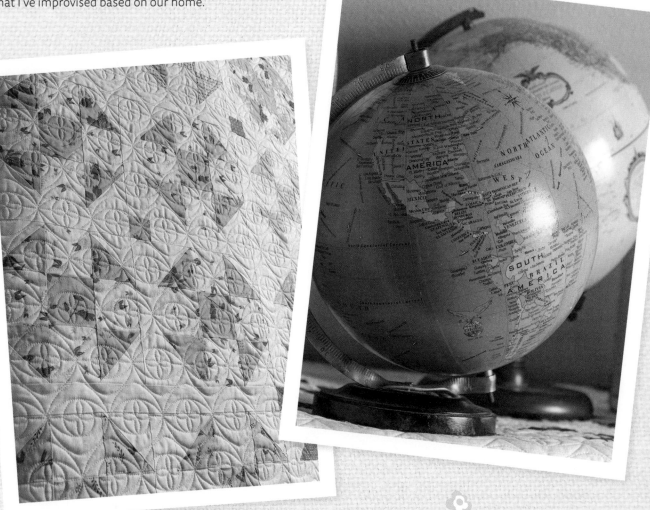

IF YOU DON'T DESIGN YOUR OWN LIFE PLAN, CHANCES ARE YOU'LL FALL INTO SOMEONE ELSE'S PLAN. AND GUESS WHAT THEY HAVE PLANNED FOR YOU? NOT MUCH.
—JIM ROHN

Project Planners

Plenty of pages for you
to track your projects!

Project Planner

This is where the fun really begins for many of us: Making a plan for the next projects on your list. Reading through the pattern and making a list of what you have and what you still need to get. Maybe you're heading to a retreat and need to make sure you don't leave without all your supplies for a project. Or perhaps you're settling in for a long weekend of sewing and don't want to be interrupted by a trip out for supplies. Whatever your circumstance, before you begin a new project, take the time to make a plan by filling out a "Project Planner." I've shared a demo of the kinds of notes and next steps I add to mine (opposite). Feel free to adapt the planners for your needs. And know there are plenty of them in the pages that follow, so you can get excited about *all* your upcoming projects!

PROJECT/PATTERN NAME

SUPPLIES

HAVE	NEED	
☑	☐	½ yard blue and white diagonal stripe for binding
☐	☑	3 yards solid cream for background
☐	☑	6 fat quarters of assorted blue prints
☑	☐	6 fat quarters of assorted red prints
☐	☐	
☐	☐	
☐	☐	
☐	☐	

QUICK TIP

At the end of a sewing session I try to leave something that can be easily put together the next time I sew. I might gather all the pieces I've cut for the next step, or trim a set of half-square triangles I know I'm going to need. The next time I pull out this project I'll have a head start since those pieces are ready to go!

QUICK TIP

To save yourself time, make a project cheat sheet. Mine usually include simplified cutting and/or sewing lists that I keep handy and store with the pattern and fabrics. That way I don't need to open up the pattern to look for the information each time.

NEXT STEPS

As you're working your way through a project, make notes of where you leave off so when you return it'll be easy to determine where to begin again.

finished all cutting; 16 block centers completed;

all 32 block centers completed; 12 of Block A completed

NOTES

Don't guess which machine setting, thread, needle, ruler, or fusible product you were using for a project. Write it down here so it's easy to remember.

Stitch Length 1.8; Aurifil 50-weight 2026 (cream);

80/12 machine needle; Mini Simple Folded Corners Ruler

FINISHED ☐

Project Planner

PROJECT/PATTERN NAME _____

_____

SUPPLIES

HAVE **NEED**

☐ ☐ _____

☐ ☐ _____

☐ ☐ _____

☐ ☐ _____

☐ ☐ _____

☐ ☐ _____

☐ ☐ _____

☐ ☐ _____

☐ ☐ _____

☐ ☐ _____

☐ ☐ _____

☐ ☐ _____

NEXT STEPS

_____

_____

_____

_____

_____

NOTES

_____

_____

_____

_____

FINISHED ☐

Project Planner

PROJECT/PATTERN NAME _____

_____

SUPPLIES

HAVE	NEED	
☐	☐	_____
☐	☐	_____
☐	☐	_____
☐	☐	_____
☐	☐	_____
☐	☐	_____
☐	☐	_____
☐	☐	_____
☐	☐	_____
☐	☐	_____
☐	☐	_____
☐	☐	_____

NEXT STEPS

_____

_____

_____

_____

_____

NOTES

_____

_____

_____

_____

FINISHED ☐

Project Planner

PROJECT/PATTERN NAME
_____

_____

SUPPLIES

HAVE NEED

☐ ☐ _____

☐ ☐ _____

☐ ☐ _____

☐ ☐ _____

☐ ☐ _____

☐ ☐ _____

☐ ☐ _____

☐ ☐ _____

☐ ☐ _____

☐ ☐ _____

☐ ☐ _____

☐ ☐ _____

NEXT STEPS

_____

_____

_____

_____

_____

_____

NOTES

_____

_____

_____

_____

FINISHED ☐

Project Planner

PROJECT/PATTERN NAME _____

_____

SUPPLIES

HAVE **NEED**

☐ ☐ _____

☐ ☐ _____

☐ ☐ _____

☐ ☐ _____

☐ ☐ _____

☐ ☐ _____

☐ ☐ _____

☐ ☐ _____

☐ ☐ _____

☐ ☐ _____

☐ ☐ _____

☐ ☐ _____

NEXT STEPS

_____

_____

_____

_____

_____

NOTES

_____

_____

_____

FINISHED ☐

Project Planner

PROJECT/PATTERN NAME

_____

_____

SUPPLIES

HAVE	NEED	
☐	☐	_____
☐	☐	_____
☐	☐	_____
☐	☐	_____
☐	☐	_____
☐	☐	_____
☐	☐	_____
☐	☐	_____
☐	☐	_____
☐	☐	_____
☐	☐	_____
☐	☐	_____

NEXT STEPS

_____

_____

_____

_____

NOTES

_____

_____

_____

_____

FINISHED ☐

Project Planner

PROJECT/PATTERN NAME

SUPPLIES

HAVE   **NEED**

☐   ☐
☐   ☐
☐   ☐
☐   ☐
☐   ☐
☐   ☐
☐   ☐
☐   ☐
☐   ☐
☐   ☐
☐   ☐

NEXT STEPS

NOTES

FINISHED ☐

Project Planner

PROJECT/PATTERN NAME

_____

_____

SUPPLIES

HAVE   NEED

☐   ☐   _____

☐   ☐   _____

☐   ☐   _____

☐   ☐   _____

☐   ☐   _____

☐   ☐   _____

☐   ☐   _____

☐   ☐   _____

☐   ☐   _____

☐   ☐   _____

☐   ☐   _____

☐   ☐   _____

NEXT STEPS

_____

_____

_____

_____

_____

NOTES

_____

_____

_____

_____

FINISHED ☐

Project Planner

PROJECT/PATTERN NAME

SUPPLIES

HAVE NEED

NEXT STEPS

NOTES

FINISHED ☐

Project Planner

PROJECT/PATTERN NAME
_____

_____

SUPPLIES

HAVE	NEED	
☐	☐	_____
☐	☐	_____
☐	☐	_____
☐	☐	_____
☐	☐	_____
☐	☐	_____
☐	☐	_____
☐	☐	_____
☐	☐	_____
☐	☐	_____
☐	☐	_____

NEXT STEPS

_____

_____

_____

_____

_____

NOTES

_____

_____

_____

_____

FINISHED ☐

Project Planner

PROJECT/PATTERN NAME _____

SUPPLIES

HAVE	NEED	
☐	☐	_____
☐	☐	_____
☐	☐	_____
☐	☐	_____
☐	☐	_____
☐	☐	_____
☐	☐	_____
☐	☐	_____
☐	☐	_____
☐	☐	_____
☐	☐	_____
☐	☐	_____

NEXT STEPS

_____
_____
_____
_____
_____
_____

NOTES

_____
_____
_____
_____

FINISHED ☐

Project Planner

PROJECT/PATTERN NAME _____

_____

SUPPLIES

HAVE	NEED	
☐	☐	_____
☐	☐	_____
☐	☐	_____
☐	☐	_____
☐	☐	_____
☐	☐	_____
☐	☐	_____
☐	☐	_____
☐	☐	_____
☐	☐	_____
☐	☐	_____
☐	☐	_____

NEXT STEPS

_____

_____

_____

_____

NOTES

_____

_____

_____

FINISHED ☐

Project Planner

PROJECT/PATTERN NAME _____

SUPPLIES

HAVE	NEED	
☐	☐	_____
☐	☐	_____
☐	☐	_____
☐	☐	_____
☐	☐	_____
☐	☐	_____
☐	☐	_____
☐	☐	_____
☐	☐	_____
☐	☐	_____
☐	☐	_____

NEXT STEPS

_____
_____
_____
_____
_____

NOTES

_____
_____
_____
_____

FINISHED ☐

Project Planner

PROJECT/PATTERN NAME
_____

SUPPLIES

HAVE **NEED**
☐ ☐ _____
☐ ☐ _____
☐ ☐ _____
☐ ☐ _____
☐ ☐ _____
☐ ☐ _____
☐ ☐ _____
☐ ☐ _____
☐ ☐ _____
☐ ☐ _____
☐ ☐ _____
☐ ☐ _____

NEXT STEPS
_____
_____
_____
_____
_____

NOTES
_____
_____
_____
_____

FINISHED ☐

Project Planner

PROJECT/PATTERN NAME

_____

SUPPLIES

HAVE | NEED

☐ ☐ _____
☐ ☐ _____
☐ ☐ _____
☐ ☐ _____
☐ ☐ _____
☐ ☐ _____
☐ ☐ _____
☐ ☐ _____
☐ ☐ _____
☐ ☐ _____
☐ ☐ _____
☐ ☐ _____

NEXT STEPS

_____
_____
_____
_____
_____
_____

NOTES

_____
_____
_____
_____

FINISHED ☐

Project Planner

PROJECT/PATTERN NAME _____

_____

SUPPLIES

HAVE	NEED	
☐	☐	_____
☐	☐	_____
☐	☐	_____
☐	☐	_____
☐	☐	_____
☐	☐	_____
☐	☐	_____
☐	☐	_____
☐	☐	_____
☐	☐	_____
☐	☐	_____
☐	☐	_____

NEXT STEPS

_____

_____

_____

_____

_____

NOTES

_____

_____

_____

_____

FINISHED ☐

Project Planner

PROJECT/PATTERN NAME

_____

_____

SUPPLIES

HAVE NEED

☐ ☐ _____

☐ ☐ _____

☐ ☐ _____

☐ ☐ _____

☐ ☐ _____

☐ ☐ _____

☐ ☐ _____

☐ ☐ _____

☐ ☐ _____

☐ ☐ _____

☐ ☐ _____

☐ ☐ _____

NEXT STEPS

_____

_____

_____

_____

_____

_____

NOTES

_____

_____

_____

_____

FINISHED ☐

Project Planner

PROJECT/PATTERN NAME
_____
_____

SUPPLIES

HAVE   **NEED**

☐ ☐ _____
☐ ☐ _____
☐ ☐ _____
☐ ☐ _____
☐ ☐ _____
☐ ☐ _____
☐ ☐ _____
☐ ☐ _____
☐ ☐ _____
☐ ☐ _____
☐ ☐ _____
☐ ☐ _____

NEXT STEPS

_____
_____
_____
_____
_____

NOTES

_____
_____
_____
_____
_____ FINISHED ☐

Project Planner

PROJECT/PATTERN NAME _____

SUPPLIES

HAVE	NEED	
☐	☐	_____
☐	☐	_____
☐	☐	_____
☐	☐	_____
☐	☐	_____
☐	☐	_____
☐	☐	_____
☐	☐	_____
☐	☐	_____
☐	☐	_____
☐	☐	_____
☐	☐	_____

NEXT STEPS

_____

_____

_____

_____

_____

NOTES

_____

_____

_____

FINISHED ☐

_____

Project Planner

PROJECT/PATTERN NAME
_____

_____

SUPPLIES

HAVE   NEED

☐   ☐   _____
☐   ☐   _____
☐   ☐   _____
☐   ☐   _____
☐   ☐   _____
☐   ☐   _____
☐   ☐   _____
☐   ☐   _____
☐   ☐   _____
☐   ☐   _____
☐   ☐   _____
☐   ☐   _____

NEXT STEPS

_____

_____

_____

_____

_____

_____

NOTES

_____

_____

_____

_____

_____

FINISHED

Project Planner

PROJECT/PATTERN NAME _____

SUPPLIES

HAVE   NEED
☐   ☐   _____
☐   ☐   _____
☐   ☐   _____
☐   ☐   _____
☐   ☐   _____
☐   ☐   _____
☐   ☐   _____
☐   ☐   _____
☐   ☐   _____
☐   ☐   _____
☐   ☐   _____
☐   ☐   _____

NEXT STEPS

_____
_____
_____
_____
_____

NOTES

_____
_____
_____
_____

FINISHED ☐

Project Planner

PROJECT/PATTERN NAME

SUPPLIES

HAVE **NEED**

☐ ☐
☐ ☐
☐ ☐
☐ ☐
☐ ☐
☐ ☐
☐ ☐
☐ ☐
☐ ☐
☐ ☐
☐ ☐
☐ ☐

NEXT STEPS

NOTES

FINISHED

Project Planner

ROJECT/PATTERN NAME _____

UPPLIES

HAVE   NEED

☐   ☐   _____

☐   ☐   _____

☐   ☐   _____

☐   ☐   _____

☐   ☐   _____

☐   ☐   _____

☐   ☐   _____

☐   ☐   _____

☐   ☐   _____

☐   ☐   _____

☐   ☐   _____

☐   ☐

XT STEPS

_____

_____

_____

_____

_____

_____

_____

TES

_____

_____

_____

_____

FINISHED ☐

Project Planner

PROJECT/PATTERN NAME

_____

_____

SUPPLIES

HAVE	NEED	
☐	☐	_____
☐	☐	_____
☐	☐	_____
☐	☐	_____
☐	☐	_____
☐	☐	_____
☐	☐	_____
☐	☐	_____
☐	☐	_____
☐	☐	_____
☐	☐	_____

NEXT STEPS

_____

_____

_____

_____

_____

NOTES

_____

_____

_____

_____

FINISHED ☐

Helpful Resources

Discover some of Sherri's
go-to supplies and reading favorites.
Plus, there's space to record your
own faves too!

Sherri's Favorite Notions & Tools

As a pattern and fabric designer, I'm often asked what my go-to quilting tools and notions are. Below, you'll find a list of my top choices. In some cases I prefer a specific brand, and in others I've listed a size or type of notion that I use often but don't have a preferred brand. It's a long list, but these are the time-tested Items I use regularly. Where there's no specific manufacturer listed, that simply means it is an important item to have on hand. Beginning quilters might find this list most helpful as they begin to add tools and notions. If you're a more seasoned quilter, I hope you'll discover a new tool here to make your quilting easier and more enjoyable.

PINS AND NEEDLES

» Clover appliqué pins
» Taylor Seville Comfort Grip Magic Pins
» 80/12 needles for machine piecing
» Size 10 Straw needles for hand stitching
» Binding needles from Primitive Gatherings

THREADS AND MACHINE FEET

» 50-weight Aurifil thread in colors 2026 (cream) and 2000 (beige)
» Sewing machine feet: ¼" foot for piecing, walking foot for machine quilting, darning foot for free-motion quilting, Teflon foot for sewing vinyl

RULERS

» Quilters Select 6" × 12"
» Creative Grids 8½" × 12½"
» Creative Grids 8½" × 24½"
» Creative Grids 4½" × 8½"
» 12½" square ruler
» ½"-wide ruler (for marking ¼" seamlines on either side of a drawn line)
» Fit to be Quarter ruler
» Simple Folded Corners and Simple Folded Corners Mini
» Bloc Loc Flying Geese rulers

CUTTING MATS

» Olfa 24" × 36" Mat in navy blue
» Olfa 12" × 17" and 17" × 24" Folding Mats
» Olfa Rotating Mat (square)
» Matilda's Own Rotating Mat (round)

SPECIALTY NOTIONS

» Clover Seam Ripper
» Clover Wonder Clips (especially handy when sewing zippers or vinyl)
» Design boards (to keep block parts and pieces organized and ready for chain piecing.)
» Alphabitties (for labeling block parts and pieces; use with Wonder Clips)
» Flatter Spray (starch alternative)
» Bobbin storage donut
» Clover Chalk Marker
» The Container Store Measuring Tape (for measuring quilt centers before cutting borders)
» Sewline Pencil
» Diagonal Seam Tape from Cluck Cluck Sew
» Triangle Paper from Primitive Gatherings

Top Tips I Want to Remember

Scratch the scratch paper and sticky notes! Keep track of the important tips you learn and don't want to forget by writing them in your planner. Jot down ideas you learn in class or read online or hear from a friend. Refer to these tips time and again until they become habits.

Press your binding away from your quilt top after machine stitching and before stitching to the back of your quilt. This results in a crisp finish for your quilt. —Sherri McConnell

Sherri's Favorite Reading Lists

Online resources are great search tools for discovering things, but I still treasure books for doing a deeper dive—for both inspiration and information. Books let you dream with your eyes open, and they're handy to highlight, flag, and return to time and again to reinforce your learning. The following lists are some of my favorites, and I've included a brief description of why I turn to them again and again.

QUILTING BOOKS SHERRI LOVES

» *Sunday Best Quilts* by Sherri McConnell and Corey Yoder (Truly a fun read with a conversation that goes on throughout the book. I'm amazed at how beautifully the projects came together, since Corey and I kept so much to ourselves until the end.)

» *Labor of Love* by Sherri McConnell (Some of my favorite techniques are included with projects ranging from simple to more complex—and the loveliest photography.)

» *Home & Hearth* by Sherri McConnell (More projects in a variety of sizes and styles with gorgeous inspirational photos.)

» *Oh, Scrap!*, *Sisterhood of Scraps*, and *Scrap School* by Lissa Alexander (All three books read like you're sitting next to Lissa having a conversation. Lots of tips included as well!)

» *Pin Pals* by Carrie Nelson (She's the ultimate pincushion authority!)

» *Sampler Spree* by Susan Ache (You'll be inspired by all 100 of these delightful 6" blocks with a unique but simple setting arrangement.)

» All the Moda All-Stars compilation books (You won't be disappointed at the number of fun projects included in each and the royalties go to charities every time!)

IN THE CASE OF GOOD BOOKS, THE POINT IS NOT TO SEE
HOW MANY OF THEM YOU CAN GET THROUGH, BUT HOW MANY
CAN GET THROUGH TO YOU. —MORTIMER J. ADLER

SHERRI'S FAVORITE ORGANIZING TIME MANAGEMENT RESOURCES

Essentialism by Greg McKeown (This book helps me discern what I want my life to be about. I've read it multiple times.)

Effortless by Greg McKeown (The follow-up to *Essentialism*, it includes so many wonderful ideas for making things work without creating more stress in your life.)

The One Thing by Gary Keller and Jay Papasan (This is a how-to book for getting focused.)

The Home Edit by Clea Shearer and Joanna Teplin (You'll find ideas for organizing every part of your home.)

Getting Things Done and *The Getting Things Done Workbook* by David Allan (Read the author's full system in the book and then work through his practical tips and techniques with the workbook)

The Paper Solution by Lisa Woodruff (The best book on paper organizing I've found. I also love Lisa's Sunday Basket System technique and use my own version of that since reading her book.)

The Lazy Genius Way by Kendra Adachi (Great ideas for simplifying and making decisions once, instead of over and over.)

Deep Work by Cal Newport (A wonderful book on what we need to do to get our best work done without interruptions.)

168 Hours by Laura Vanderkam (Terrific ideas for managing your time including time-tracking, which has helped me pinpoint how long projects will take.)

Outer Order, Inner Calm by Gretchen Rubin (An organizing book with so many simple takeaways.)

Free to Focus by Michael Hyatt (Designed for work and business, Michael Hyatt's systems make so much sense.)

SHERRI'S FAVORITE INSPIRATIONAL BOOKS (NONFICTION)

» *Little Farmstead Living* by Julie Thomas (A treasury of inspirational photos and ideas for those who dream of a country life in the city.)

» *Homebody* by Joanna Gaines (Design information and inspiration you can incorporate into your own home and style.)

» *The Happiness Project* by Gretchen Rubin (It's filled with great ideas on positivity and realizing true happiness.)

» *The Gifts of Imperfection* by Brené Brown (People tend to be too hard on themselves, and the wisdom in this book helps me give myself grace and understanding.)

» *Atomic Habits* by James Clear (Inspirational stories and solid advice on the importance of habit is the key here.)

» *Grit* by Angela Duckworth (Full of practical advice and wisdom, this look at successful individuals is inspiring.)

» *Gift from the Sea* by Anne Morrow Lindbergh (A classic, it inspires me to take time to slow down and enjoy the process of creativity.)

My Book Must-Haves

Keep a running list of your latest book acquisitions (quilting books and others) along with your "Wish List." You won't have to wonder whether you have that new release—and you'll have recommendations at the ready when family members ask you for gift ideas!

HAVE	WANT	TITLE
☐	☐	
☐	☐	
☐	☐	
☐	☐	
☐	☐	
☐	☐	
☐	☐	
☐	☐	
☐	☐	
☐	☐	
☐	☐	
☐	☐	
☐	☐	
☐	☐	
☐	☐	
☐	☐	
☐	☐	
☐	☐	
☐	☐	
☐	☐	
☐	☐	
☐	☐	

HAVE	WANT	TITLE
☐	☐	
☐	☐	
☐	☐	
☐	☐	
☐	☐	
☐	☐	
☐	☐	
☐	☐	
☐	☐	
☐	☐	
☐	☐	
☐	☐	
☐	☐	
☐	☐	

ALWAYS BEAR IN MIND THAT
YOUR OWN RESOLUTION TO
SUCCEED IS MORE IMPORTANT
THAN ANY OTHER ONE THING.
—ABRAHAM LINCOLN

About the Author

As a quilt and fabric designer, I make many quilts, pillows, runners, and bags each year.

I make them to showcase the latest fabrics in each Sherri & Chelsi collection for Moda Fabrics. Frequently, I design quilts for magazines and books. And last but certainly not least, I enjoy making quilts for my family and friends.

I'm fortunate to have a business that revolves around our shared love of quilting and to work with my daughter Chelsi to design fabrics. But having a long quilting to-do list makes it a must for me to stay organized so I can meet all my deadlines. That need to stay on track while still enjoying the process has led to my passion for finding the best and easiest ways to get—and stay—organized.

I hope the information, lists, and suggestions in this planner and workbook will help you find joy in quilting each and every day.